MONKEYS

Gibbons

Mae Woods
ABDO & Daughters

visit us at
www.abdopub.com

Published by Abdo & Daughters, 4940 Viking Drive, Suite 622, Edina, Minnesota 55435.

Copyright © 1998 by Abdo Consulting Group, Inc., Pentagon Tower, P.O. Box 36036, Minneapolis, Minnesota 55435 USA. International copyrights reserved in all countries. No part of this book may be reproduced in any form without written permission from the publisher.

Printed in the United States.

Cover Photo credits: Peter Arnold, Inc.
Interior Photo credits: Peter Arnold, Inc.

Edited by Lori Kinstad Pupeza

Library of Congress Cataloging-in-Publication Data

Woods, Mae.
    Gibbons / Mae Woods.
    p. cm. -- (Monkeys)
    Includes index.
    Summary: Describes the physical characteristics and behavior of these Lesser Apes that live in the rain forest of Malaysia, Thailand, and Southeast Asia.
    ISBN 1-56239-598-X
    1. Gibbons--Juvenile literature. [1. Gibbons.] I. Title. II. Series: Woods, Mae. Monkeys.
    QL737.P96W644   1998
    599.88'2--dc20
                                        96-11379
                                         CIP
                                       AC

Contents

Gibbons

Gibbons are in the same ape family as **gorillas**, **orangutans**, and **chimpanzees**. These three are called Great Apes. Gibbons are called Lesser Apes because they are smaller and their brains are not as large as the other apes.

Gibbons look like monkeys and have some of the same **features**. But gibbons do not have tails, and they are apes rather than monkeys.

Apes and monkeys live to be about 35 or 40 years old. Apes, monkeys, and humans are **primates**. This is the highest order in the animal world.

Opposite page: A white-haired Gibbon.

Where They Live

Gibbons live in the rain forests of Malaysia, Thailand, and Southeast Asia. Animals from different areas **vary** in color and looks. These are divided into different **species**.

There are nine species of gibbons. The **lar** gibbon is the most unusual looking. It has a white ruff of fur surrounding its face and white fur on its hands and feet.

The **siamang** gibbon is the largest. It lives in Sumatra and Malaysia. It is twice as large as other types of gibbons, weighing as much as 40 pounds. It is all black. Both males and females have a throat pouch like the male **orangutan**.

When the siamang calls or sings, the pouch enlarges so it can make very loud sounds.

Southeast Asia

Australia

6

A siamang gibbon from Malaysia.

What They Are Like

Gibbons live in trees. They are sometimes called "tree walkers" for their amazing **skill** in leaping from branch to branch like **acrobats**.

Gibbons come in many different colors: pale yellow, black, gray, brown-gray, or gold. In some **species** the males and females have different coloring. There are even some kinds of gibbons that change colors as they grow older.

They have soft, thick coats of fur that protect them from the rain. They have small, round faces and large, sharp teeth.

Opposite page: An endangered black gibbon in a tree.

Size and Strength

Male and female gibbons are the same size. They weigh about 15 pounds (6.8 kg) and stand up to 3 feet tall (.9 m). Gibbons have hands with long, hook-like fingers, but no thumbs. But on their feet, they have big toes that move just like thumbs. They can grasp branches and objects with their toes. They use their feet to do many of the things other animals do with their hands.

Gibbons have **muscular** legs and arms. They can stand and walk upright on two legs. But they like to do this in the trees rather than on the ground. They can also walk on vines just like tightrope walkers at the circus. To keep their balance, they hold their long arms over their heads or crossed behind their necks.

Gibbons cannot walk on all fours because their arms are too long. They can climb trees on all fours like squirrels do. They can move faster than any monkey or ape.

Like other apes, gibbons sleep in the trees. They do not build sleeping nests. They perch in the forks of large branches, hunch over, and wrap their long arms around their bodies. They have thick pads of skin on their backside to act as cushions. They are comfortable sitting for hours in this **position**.

Gibbons have strong arms that help them climb trees and balance on branches.

Gibbon Families

Gibbons live in families with one mother, one father, and two or three young ones. The parents are devoted to each other and remain partners for life. Gibbons are the only apes that have single families. All of the other animals live in larger groups and have more than one mate.

Gibbon family members are **affectionate**. They embrace one another in greeting and seem to enjoy being together. Once a gibbon family claims its own fruit trees, it will not share the area. They are not friendly with other gibbons when it is time to eat or sleep.

A special **skill** that gibbons have is their ability to **vocalize**. They sing and make sounds to **communicate** with each other.

*Gibbons are affectionate animals that like
to play with each other.*

A Gibbon Song

Gibbons begin each day with a song. When they wake up, the family gathers together and the father sings out a special gibbon call. When he is finished, the mother **performs** a song of her own. Then the young gibbons join in.

After singing for awhile, they stop and wait for a response from another family. From the distance, other gibbons will call out in the same way. Then the first family will sing again in reply. This morning song goes on for about 15 minutes.

In this way, gibbons show all the animals where they are and how large their family is. After singing, the gibbons swing through the trees to find something to eat for breakfast.

Opposite page: A white handed gibbon looking for food.

The "Great Call"

In the afternoon, there is a "great call" that the female makes. It is even louder than the father's morning song. She will sing alone for several minutes before he joins in.

Gibbons sing and make many other sounds throughout the day. Each sound is unique and has a different meaning. They give a little hoot so they will not lose sight of each other in the trees. They call out when they are upset or to warn of danger. They shout when they first see food. This is a happy sound.

Baby gibbons have their own calls. They grunt and squeal as they play. There is a special sound they make when they want their parents. Parents always know their own baby's cry. No two babies sound alike to their mother or father.

A dark handed gibbon in Borneo, an Island in Asia.

Food

Gibbons like to eat fruit. Figs are their favorite food. They also eat grapes, plums, flowers, leaves, and insects. Usually they eat in the trees, using one arm to hang on the limb. They use their feet or their other hand to pick the fruit.

They come down from the trees to find water. They drink water by dipping their hands in a stream and licking off the liquid. They can also suck water off the leaves after it rains.

The male gibbon always leads the family on its food search. Sometimes he carries the baby to help the mother. When gibbons eat, they carefully look at the food and chew it slowly. Meals last a long time. After eating, the family will rest or **groom** each other.

A gibbon family will allow other animals to share their fruit trees, but not other gibbons. If two families approach the same fruit, the male gibbons hoot and shriek at one another and stomp on the branches. They do not usually fight. Whoever makes the most noise claims the spot. The other family will move on to find another tree.

Gibbons use their climbing skills to find fruit to eat.

Babies

Gibbon babies are tiny when they are born. They are about the size of a mouse. They grow quickly but they are very **dependent** on their mothers during their first year.

The baby drinks its mother's milk and nestles in her lap. She wraps her arms around it to protect it and keep it warm. In a few months the infant is able to clasp its arms around its mother's waist and swing through the trees with her.

Gibbons are devoted parents. Both parents like to **groom** their baby and play with it. Some fathers will carry the young one during the day and let it sleep with its mother at night.

At four months old, the baby begins to learn to climb and hang by its feet. It wants to play with its older brothers and sisters. While their parents nap in the afternoon, the young gibbons chase each other or wrestle. They never stray too far away from their family.

When gibbons are two years old, they are able to look after themselves. They will stay with their parents until age five. Then they are ready to go off and start a family of their own.

A mother gibbon with her young.

Glossary

acrobats - Performers who do tricks on the trapeze or tightrope.

affectionate (a-FEK-shun-it) - A friendly feeling; fondness; love.

chimpanzee (chim-pan-ZEE) - A small, dark-haired ape from Africa.

communicate (kuh-mew-nih-KATE) - To express thoughts.

dependent - Relying on someone else for help.

features - Special qualities or parts.

gorilla (guh-RIL-uh) - A large African ape with a thick body and dark hair.

groom - To clean and care for.

lar - A gibbon with white markings on its face, hands and feet.

muscular (MUS-kyoo-ler) - Made up of muscles; strong.

orangutan (uh-RANG-uh-tan) - A red-haired ape found in Southeast Asia.

performs - Doing something that requires skill.

position - The way a person or thing is placed.

primates (PRIE-maytz) - A group of animals, which includes humans, apes, and monkeys.

siamang - The largest gibbon.

skill - Ability.

species (SPEE-sheez) - A group of animals that are alike in certain ways.

vary - To differ.

vocalize - To make sounds; to sing.

Index